**DO NOT REMOVE
CARDS FROM POCKET**

WORLD WAR TWO

LIFE IN THE THIRD REICH

PETER NEVILLE

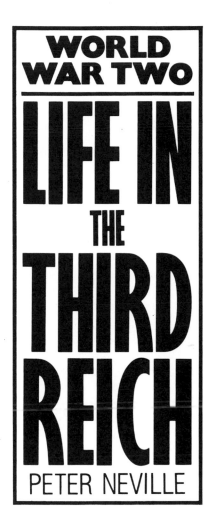

WORLD WAR TWO

LIFE IN THE THIRD REICH

PETER NEVILLE

B. T. BATSFORD · LONDON

Typeset by Latimer Trend & Co Ltd, Plymouth
and printed in Great Britain by
Butler and Tanner, Frome, Somerset
Published by B. T. Batsford Ltd, 4 Fitzhardinge
Street, London W1H 0AH

A CIP catalogue record for this book is available from the British Library.

ISBN 0 7134 6542 5

CONTENTS

ACKNOWLEDGMENTS

The Author and Publishers would like to thank the following for permission to reproduce illustrations: Barnaby's Picture Library for pages 11, 24, 32 and 47; The Bundesarchivs for pages 43 and 45a; The Mary Evans Picture Library for page 9; The Hulton Picture Library for pages 31 and 41; The Keystone Collection for pages 28 and 44; Peter Newark's Military Pictures for pages 18 and 51; Popperfoto for pages 8, 13, 15, 16, 17, 19, 22, 29, 30, 45b, 50, 54a, 55 and 56; The Wiener Library for page 25.

The cover illustrations show a Nazi rally of 1933 (courtesy of Barnaby's Picture Library), and in colour, a propaganda poster promoting 'youth, hostels and homes' (courtesy of the E.T. Archive).

THE NIGHT OF THE LONG KNIVES

In the early hours of 30 June 1934 a convoy of black Mercedes swept along the road from Munich in Southern Germany, to the lakeside resort of Bad Wiessee. One of these cars contained Adolf Hitler, who was about to settle scores with his old friend Ernst Röhm, the head of the brown-shirted SA (Sturm Abteilung or Storm Troopers). Meantime, Röhm and his SA cronies slept on, unaware of the fate that lay in store for them.

At 7.10 a.m., the convoy reached Bad Wiessee and black-shirted SS men (Hitler's personal bodyguard) vaulted the fence surrounding the lakeside hotel where Röhm was staying. Led by Hitler himself the SS men rushed up the stairs to Röhm's room, where the enraged Führer bellowed, 'Ernst, you are under arrest'. Röhm and many of the SA men were homosexuals and Hitler was beside himself with rage (it seemed) about the open evidence of sexual depravity. In fact he had known about Röhm's homosexuality for years. So began what the Nazi leadership called 'Operation Humming Bird', the ruthless slaughter of the SA leadership.

How was it that these two old friends and colleagues had fallen out? To answer this question we need to return to the heady days

> **I feel compelled to thank you, my dear Ernst Röhm, for the imperishable services which you have rendered to the Nationalist Socialist movement and the German people.**
>
> *Part of Hitler's New Year message to Röhm, 1934 (he also sent Röhm a bust of his mother!)*

of 30 January 1933 when Hitler and the Nazi Party had taken power in Germany, although at that stage they had to share it with others. That very evening Adolf Hitler, as Führer and Chancellor, reviewed a torchlight procession of his SA from the balcony of the old imperial chancellery, while the senile old President Hindenburg wondered if the demonstrators were 'all Russian prisoners'. All this was to be expected. For years, after all, the 'brown trash', as their enemies called them, had kicked communist heads and smashed up socialist meeting halls for 'the Führer and the Fatherland'. This was their reward.

At the time it seemed that Ernst Röhm, the scarred ex-army officer who had marched

Brownshirt leader Ernst Röhm. On his left is SS chief Heinrich Himmler.

with Hitler during the failed 'Beerhall' rising of 1923, was the second most powerful man in Germany. He commanded four million devoted Brownshirts, and answered to no one but Adolf Hitler himself. As the Nazis destroyed German democracy in 1933, Ernst Röhm and his Brownshirts were in the forefront. They set up the first concentration camp at Dachau. You can still visit the remains of the old concentration camp at Dachau, or the 'Brownhouse' in Munich where many SA men were taken on 30 June 1934. They helped round up the communists, socialists, and trade unionists the Nazis hated, and swaggered around the streets of Berlin beating up Jews, and smashing their shop windows.

> **What that ridiculous corporal says means nothing to us.**
>
> *Ernst Röhm on Hitler in 1934*

But Ernst Röhm then began to overreach himself. He started to talk about a 'Second Revolution' which would break the power of the big factory bosses and the landowners in Germany. Worse, he started saying that the Brownshirts must be merged with the army to form one fighting force. This infuriated the generals who told Hitler that Röhm must be silenced. They had no intention of allowing the 'brown trash' to share their privileges and social status. Hitler was threatened with a military takeover, and he knew he couldn't stay in power without army support. He also knew that he needed the support of the industrialists, bankers and landowners who had helped to put him in power. So the SA had to be dealt with.

> **I want my SA leaders to be men not ridiculous apes.**
>
> *Adolf Hitler, 1934*

Propaganda poster showing Brownshirts 'Fighting the terror of the left'.

A secret meeting, probably on the pocket battleship *Deutschland* took place in the spring of 1934, between Hitler and the army leaders, and a straightforward deal was arranged. Hitler would deal with Röhm and the SA. The army for its part would promise loyalty to the Nazi government, and get the guns and tanks needed for German rearmament.

There was one minor hiccup on the road to 'Operation Humming Bird'. It centred around the unlikely figure of Franz von Papen, the Vice Chancellor in the German government, and old President Hindenburg's favourite. It was Papen who had persuaded Hindenburg to make Hitler Chancellor, foolishly thinking that he, Papen, would hold the real power. Belatedly, Papen made a speech in mid June at Marburg, in which he dared to criticize the Nazi government. Hitler was furious, and told his Propaganda Minister Josef Goebbels to make sure that the speech didn't get into the newspapers.

> **It is time to join together in fraternal friendship and respect for all our fellow countrymen, to avoid disturbing the labours of serious men and to silence fanatics.**
>
> *Part of Papen's Marburg speech, June 1934*

By now the framework of a plan for dealing with the SA was appearing. Hermann Goering, the head of the Luftwaffe (Air Force) and Gestapo (standing for Geheime Staats Politizei or Secret State Police) was to be the planner, and Heinrich Himmler, the sinister head of the SS, the executioner. Lists were drawn up, not just of SA leaders but of anyone the Nazi leadership wanted to be rid of. 30 June 1934 was chosen to be the day for 'Operation Humming Bird'.

Did Hitler have second thoughts about killing his old ally? He was certainly in a highly nervous state in those late June days, but he knew he had no choice. On 21 June President Hindenburg told the jumpy Chancellor that Röhm had to be crushed or else. The Brownshirts had already been sent on extended leave for the whole month of July.

THE NIGHT OF THE LONG KNIVES

Great efforts were made in those last days to keep the plan a secret. Goering even went to the wedding of the SA chief in Berlin, although this man was on the death list. Then the blow was struck, as silently and ruthlessly as it had been planned.

> **Sepp, my friend, what on earth is happening?**
>
> *Brownshirt leader August Schneidhuber to his old SS friend Sepp Dietrich before he was shot.*

SA leaders were rounded up all over Germany. One was seized as he was about to start a honeymoon cruise, and like many of his colleagues, he died shouting 'Heil Hitler', without ever understanding what was happening. Many SA men, including Röhm himself, were taken to the Lichterfelde Barracks in Berlin for execution. Röhm was given the choice of shooting himself but is said to have replied, 'If I am to be killed, let Adolf do it himself.' Two SS men carried out the execution.

> **All revolutions devour their own children.**
>
> *Ernst Röhm, 30 June 1934*

Gregor Strasser, another leading Nazi from the old days, also died at the Lichterfelde under a hail of bullets. He had once dared to oppose Hitler's ideas. The 'Night of the Long Knives' was a time for settling old scores, stretching right back to 1923. Gustav von Kahr, the Bavarian prime minister who had failed to support the Beerhall uprising was executed, but so (strangely) was the Catholic priest who had read the proofs of Hitler's book *Mein Kampf*. The most famous victim other than Röhm was General Kurt von Schleicher, Germany's last Chancellor before Hitler. Schleicher (in English his name means 'Creeper', a good name for this devious political general) was at home answering a telephone call. His cook showed two visitors into Schleicher's study. 'Are you General von Schleicher?' one of the visitors asked. 'Yes,' replied Schleicher who was then gunned down on the spot (his wife was shot immediately afterwards). The army generals were too cowardly to ask for a proper enquiry into Schleicher's murder.

The Imperial War Museum screens Programme One in 'The World at War' series (Thames TV) on Nazi Germany. It is also available on video.

And so it went on. Even von Papen was placed under house arrest, and probably only saved because he lived in a road full of foreign reporters and ambassadors. Even the Nazis thought twice about slaughtering Germany's Vice Chancellor in full public view. His aides were not so lucky. One escaped only by jumping over his garden wall, as a truckload of SS arrived outside. Another, who had helped to write the Marburg speech, was shot dead in his office.

Hermann Goering.

> **In one of the rooms I saw a large pool of dried blood on the floor. There, on June 30, Herbert von Bose, one of Papen's assistants, had been shot.**
>
> *Albert Speer, then Hitler's architect, and later his Armaments Minister*

Official excuses were put forward for the 'Night of the Long Knives'. Röhm was a sexual degenerate (a fact always denied by his family) who had been planning a putsch (revolt) against Hitler. Schleicher was alleged to have been conspiring with the French against Germany.

> **In the last analysis, a little man.**
>
> *Röhm's sister-in-law talking about Hitler in 1980*

There were, of course, mistakes, so great was the bloodshed. In Munich, a music critic called Dr Willy Schmid was mistaken for a local Brownshirt leader called Wilhelm Schmid, and taken away to be executed. Later Hitler's deputy Rudolf Hess visited the unfortunate widow, ordered her to keep her mouth shut, and arranged for her to receive a pension. These facts only became known after World War Two.

> **You boys like a story, well I'm going to give you a story!**
>
> *Goering, gloating before the foreign press at the press conference after 30 June.*

Hitler was nervous about the blood purge, but he excused himself before the Reichstag (parliament) and duly received the thanks of the 85 year old President Hindenburg, who sent his 'profound thanks and sincere appre-

ciation'. Never again was the SA a threat to Hitler's power, and after June 1934 it was subordinated to the SS.

> **A visit to the British newspaper Library at Colindale (North London) will help to understand the British reaction.**

Foreign opinion was shocked by the 'Night of the Long Knives', but it was seen to be a German domestic matter. The British ambassador had warned his government in 1933 that 'the persons directing the policy of the Hitler government are not normal. Many of us indeed, have a feeling that we are living in a country where fantastic hooligans and eccentrics have got the upper hands'. As you will realize by now, this description flattered the Nazis considerably.

> **I have a sense of horror when I look at that man.**
>
> *US ambassador Dodds after hearing Hitler's explanation for the 'Night of the Long Knives' before the Reichstag.*

What were the effects of 30 June inside Germany? Firstly it strengthened Hitler's own position by removing a possible rival in Röhm. Secondly, it won for Hitler the absolute loyalty of the German army. When Hindenburg, the old war hero, died in August, Adolf Hitler made every German soldier swear an oath of loyalty *not just* to Germany, but to him personally as Führer or Chief. Lastly, it made Germany a *totalitarian state* where no opposition to Nazism was allowed. Goering summed up the situation in a phrase: 'It is the Führer alone who decides.'

It is difficult to assess exactly how many people died during that one summer's night

Hitler with President Hindenburg.

in 1934. No one believed Hitler's claim that only 74 had been executed, and a figure of two hundred seems quite possible.

Views of the Night of the Long Knives. Compare what they are saying: Hitler quite openly now claimed the 'right' to rid himself of his opponents without either legal investigation or trial.

Karl Dietrich Bracher, German historian, 1970

Thousands of the most motivated Nazis would never forget the weekend of shame.

John Toland, US historian, 1976

Possibly Hitler's action did indeed avert that 'second revolution' Röhm was supposed to have been plotting. With such arguments we soothed our consciences.

Albert Speer, Memoirs, 1970

For anyone less blind than the generals, the way in which Hitler dealt with the threat of a second revolution must have brought consternation rather than satisfaction.

Alan Bullock, British historian, 1962

COUNTDOWN TO OPERATION HUMMING BIRD

1 January 1934	Hitler sends Röhm a 'friendly' New Year Message.	17 June	Papen makes his Marburg speech.
11 April	Hitler meets the generals on the battleship *Deutschland*.	21 June	Hindenburg tells Hitler to deal with the SA or risk a military takeover.
7 June	SA units sent on leave for the month of July.	30 June	Operation Humming Bird put into practice.

THE ECONOMY

Hitler promised that when he came to power he would put Germany back to work. In 1932 six million Germans were out of work. This message appealed to the workforce. He also promised to set the German economy back on its feet. This appealed to the middle classes. They had suffered very badly in the *hyperinflation* of 1923, when their savings had become worthless. No sooner did Germany recover in the late 1920s, than she was hit by a second severe depression from 1929 to 1933. Hitler, a small town boy himself, understood middle class or bourgeois insecurities.

Hitler also won over the industrialists and landowners, by saying that he would keep the workers in order. The wealthy classes were frightened of communism, and had seen how the SA battled with 'the Reds' in the streets. In economic terms then, Hitler was all things to all men—unless you happened to be a trade unionist who wanted a pay rise.

Hitler said he would lower unemployment and he did. The price he demanded was the abolition of the trade unions. They were too closely linked to the hated Weimar democracy. In destroying the unions the Führer demonstrated a sense of humour (of sorts). He made 1 May Labour Day, a national holiday. The next day he abolished the trade unions. They were replaced by a Nazi 'Labour Front', led by Robert Ley. But the Nazis had to produce results.

> **The Nazi dictatorship was not imposed in a sudden, frictionless way. It had to produce results. By the beginning of 1935 there were still three million unemployed and many others on very low wages. Not until 1936–7 was recovery established beyond doubt.**
>
> *Richard Overy, Modern History Review, 1989*

In the early 1930s the German army opened soup kitchens to feed some of the six million unemployed.

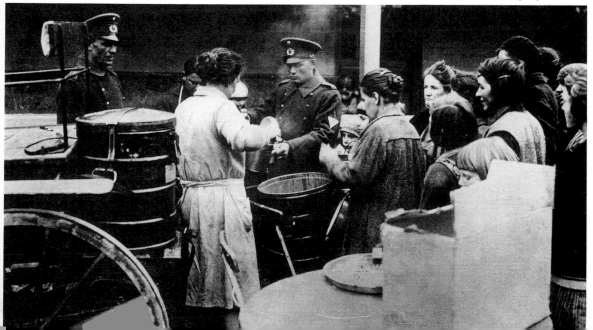

THE FOUR YEAR PLAN

Hitler put Goering in charge of a Four Year Plan to rebuild the economy. The Air Force chief was to achieve *autarky*—that is to make Germany free of dependence on foreign goods. But first came unemployment. It was lowered by a number of means:

A. Through *public works schemes*. Building roads (*autobahns* or motorways were constructed—the first in Europe), bridges, houses, clearing swamps, planting trees and so on. This took the unemployed off the streets.

B. *Rearmament*. The build-up of Germany's armed forces after 1935 created jobs in arms factories. More tanks, planes, and guns were needed.

C. *Conscription*. When Hitler increased his army (breaking the Versailles Treaty) to 300,000 men in 1935 many young men came off the unemployment register.

Only a Nazi style dictatorship could cure unemployment in this way. In Britain rearmament was a matter of controversy. But Hitler could do things without consulting anyone.

Thames TV's 'World at War' (Programme 1) and BBC Schools (World History Programme 3) provide interesting film footage on the economic recovery.

TABLE SHOWING UNEMPLOYMENT IN GERMANY 1932–7 (MILLIONS)

Year	Unemployment
1932	6.04
1933	6.01
1934	3.77
1935	2.97
1936	2.52
1937	1.85

Source: Statistical Yearbook for the German Reich 1940

Goering is associated with the phrase 'guns before butter'. In fact this is a bit misleading. True, Germany *was* rearming at a ferocious pace before 1939. But Hitler was always nervous about his popularity. So he didn't allow the standard of living of the

Hitler did much to improve the economic situation. Here he is laying the foundation stone of the first Volkswagen (People's Car) factory.

workers to be affected by rearmament too much. The 'Strength Through Joy' programme arranged cheap holiday cruises for the workers to Majorca for example (although it is true that they never got the Volkswagens [People's Cars] that Goering promised them!). There was also the 'Winterhilfe' (Winterhelp) programme to provide poor people with clothing and food.

A 'BLITZKRIEG ECONOMY'

There was another reason why the Nazis didn't put the whole economy on a war footing. Hitler had fought in the First World War, and didn't want a repetition of it. So his foreign policy aims (see Chapter 7) were to be achieved by fighting short wars, the so-called 'blitzkrieg': *Blitzkrieg* means 'lightning war', using tanks and dive bombers to win quick victories. Quick victories meant that not all of the German economy was needed for war production.

It was a plan which worked well in the years 1939–41. But it came unstuck in the snows of Russia. The Red Army wouldn't lie down and roll over before the Blitzkrieg.

Even then Hitler was most reluctant to put the whole German economy on a war footing. He was too slow to recognize the need to do so.

> **It remains one of the oddities of this war that Hitler demanded less from his people than Churchill and Roosevelt did from their respective nations. The discrepancy between the total mobilization of labour forces in democratic England and the casual treatment of this question in authoritarian Germany is proof of the regime's anxiety not to risk any shift in popular mood. The German leaders were not disposed to make sacrifices themselves or to ask sacrifices of the people.**
>
> Albert Speer, *Inside the Third Reich*, 1970

This fact was a matter of constant complaint by Hitler's Armaments Minister Albert Speer, probably the ablest man in the Nazi government. According to Speer in 1942

Workers from the Labour Corps build a stretch of Autobahn.

Germany's consumer industries (i.e. those not producing arms) were producing at a rate only 3 per cent below the peacetime level of 1939.

GERMAN WOMEN IN WARTIME

Another interesting feature of the wartime Nazi economy was its treatment of women. The Nazi party slogan was 'Kinder, Kirche, Kuche' (Child, Church and Kitchen). This meant that women should have children, go to church, and do the housework. The idea grew that German women didn't take part in the war effort, because the Nazi party wouldn't let them. This wasn't really true. Modern research shows that while in 1939 Britain had only 25 per cent of its women in warwork, Germany had 37 per cent. By 1944 the German figure was 51 per cent, the British 36 per cent. So the truth was denied by Nazi propaganda. Hitler himself would have liked German women to be like his rather easily dominated girl friend (and later wife) Eva Braun. She spent her time swimming, skiing, and reading romantic novels, while the Führer largely ignored her. Hitler claimed that he was too busy to raise a family.

Life for other German women was very different. They were meant to have lots of children. In 1939–40 German doctors were reporting many cases of depression and nervous exhaustion in the female workforce.

> **Contrary to my expectations (I still took German efficiency for granted) the rationing system in Berlin was chaotic ... 'German women, your leader and your country trust you'. Such pious slogans staring out hopefully from every other kiosk, every other billboard, made no impression whatsoever on the agile Hausfrau (housewife) hell-bent on a fruitful scavenge.**
>
> Christobel Bielenburg, The Past is Myself, Corgi Books, 1989.
>
> Christobel was an English woman married to the German Peter Bielenburg (a friend of Adam von Trott, see Chapter 5). She writes here of her experiences in wartime Nazi Germany. Her book was recently made into a BBC TV series.

All this provides a good example of how history *is not a dead subject*. Historians continue to find new documents and information about the past. In the 1950s, the view that German women were kept out of the workforce might have been believed. In the 1990s, it cannot.

GERMAN TECHNOLOGY

The Germans were great inventors. By the end of the war they had invented a jet fighter (the ME 262), a pilotless flying bomb (the

Diagram of the V1 flying bomb.

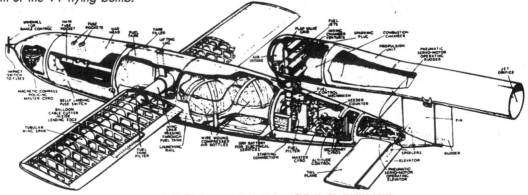

VERGELTUNGSWAFFE EINS (FZG-76)—THE V1 OR FLYING-BOMB

V1), and the V2 rocket, a forerunner of the ballistic missiles of today. They were also working on a German atomic bomb, which fortunately Hitler never got. But this technical superiority didn't work for the Germans, largely because of Hitler's prejudices. He was obsessed with producing tanks and guns, and gave low priority to submarines, jet aircraft, the V1 weapons, and the atomic project. As Albert Speer says in *Inside the Third Reich*, in matters of economic planning, Hitler was an amateur.

The BBC has produced an interesting documentary on the V weapons which is on video (colour and black and white).

The Secret War—Volume 2: Terror Weapons and It. (From BBC Video).

Hitler with Eva Braun.

It seemed far more practicable to all concerned to employ German women rather than assorted foreign labour. Businessmen came to me with statistics showing that the employment of German women during the First World War had been significantly higher than it was now. They showed me photographs of workers streaming out of the same ammunition factory at closing time in 1918 and 1942; in the earlier war they had been predominantly women: now they were almost entirely men. They had pictures from American and British magazines which indicated to what extent women were pitching in on the industrial front in those countries.

Albert Speer, Inside The Third Reich, 1970

Other women in 'consumer' industry found themselves working on war orders for uniforms and military equipment of all kinds. By 1941 almost half the output from these sectors went not to civilians but to the armed forces. Other women were left to run the family farm or shop now that the males were conscripted. While it was possible to return a skilled metalworker back to his job (and his family) to make weapons, no-one argued that farmers and shopkeepers should get the same privileges. Women worked long hours, with little help, until more foreign labour was brought in to keep agriculture going later in the war.

Richard Overy, History Review, 1989

THE ECONOMY

The Nazi reliance on slave labour also proved counterproductive. Men and women from all over the Nazi empire were forced to go and work in Germany (including some from the British Channel Islands). Many were beaten and starved to death. They all needed to be guarded by soldiers or the SS. Most couldn't speak German. Such deportations only encouraged resistance in countries like Belgium, France, Holland, Poland, and Russia

In the end the German attempt to take on the powerful US, Soviet and British economies was a disaster. Albert Speer ended up trying to flood Hitler's underground headquarters with gas, in a futile effort to shorten the war. It didn't save him from 20 years imprisonment as a war criminal in 1946.

THE RING OF TERROR: THE NAZI SECURITY SERVICES

One of the most puzzling things about Nazi Germany is how the party kept such a firm grip over people. When we learn that only 43 per cent of the people voted Nazi in 1933, it is natural to wonder about this. The answer is really quite simple. The Nazi 'terror system' was so effective, that most Germans were afraid to oppose the government. Worse, people began to betray their own friends and relatives to the authorities to save themselves.

> **Thus very early in 1933 there was the case of a Dr Kuno Ruhmann who went to a party and, after one drink too many, sought to entertain people by imitating Hitler's way of speaking. The next morning his hostess reported him to Nazi headquarters.**
>
> *William Sheridan Allen, The Nazi Seizure of Power, 1965*

THE BROWNSHIRTS

In the early days before the Night of the Long Knives, the SA played a prominent role in terrorizing the population. The Jews were an obvious target, but so too were communists and socialists. The first concentration camp at Dachau was set up to deal with the latter. The brownshirted bully boys were used to make ordinary Germans aware of the physical threat of Nazism.

After 30 June 1934 the Brownshirts were obviously much less important. But they were still part of the bullying and spying on ordinary Germans, that went on.

> **The city was full of whispers. They told of illegal midnight arrests, of prisoners tortured in the SA barracks, made to spit on Lenin's picture, swallow castor-oil, eat old socks.**
>
> *Christopher Isherwood, The Berlin Stories, 1963*

21

THE BLACKSHIRTS

After 1934 the black-shirted SS under their leader Heinrich Himmler, grew in importance and size. In 1936 Himmler got overall control of all the police organizations in Nazi Germany, except for the Abwehr (see diagram). There were also separate SS units fighting with the Army in World War Two, like the notorious Death's Head Division. But the main job of the SS was to guard the concentration camps, and supervise the murder of millions of Jews, Poles, Russians, Catholic and Protestant clergy, gypsies, and mentally retarded people. In short, all the people who didn't fit in with the Nazi world view.

The SS continued to have a variety of other jobs, like being personal bodyguards for Hitler.

HIMMLER

Heinrich Himmler was a strange man, even by the standards of the Nazi leadership. His cranky racial theories resulted in the measurement of human skulls. Every SS man (and his wife) had to have the right measurements before marriage was allowed. The aim was to produce a blond-haired race of supermen and women. Yet Himmler was dark and bespectacled. He fainted at the sight of blood, and was sick when he visited one of his own

THE NAZI SECURITY APPARATUS

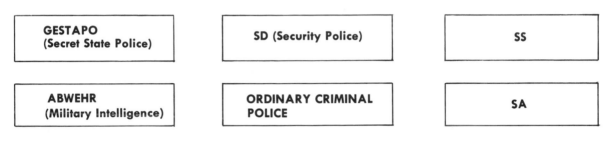

GESTAPO (Secret State Police)	**SD (Security Police)**	**SS**
ABWEHR (Military Intelligence)	**ORDINARY CRIMINAL POLICE**	**SA**

An SA and SS man stick anti-Semitic signs on Jewish shop.

death camps. Behind the mild-looking nobody, however, was the mind of one of the greatest mass murderers of the twentieth century.

> **Apart from the efficiency with which he built up his organization, he was a man of undistinguished personality and limited intelligence.**
>
> *Alan Bullock, Hitler: a Study on Tyranny, 1952*

Heydrich and the SD

Even more sinister than Heinrich Himmler in some ways was his deputy Reinhard Heydrich. Six foot and fair haired, Heydrich looked every inch an Aryan superman. He had been thrown out of the navy for getting a girl pregnant, and joined the SS. He rose rapidly through its ranks. Heydrich's special responsibility was the Sicherdienst (SD) or Security Police, which had the special task of spying on the anti-Hitler opposition. It was as ruthless as its leader.

In 1941 Heydrich was given the extra job of running Bohemia and Moravia (the *Czech* part of Czechoslovakia). The British feared that he was being groomed as Hitler's successor. So they parachuted Czech agents in with the job of killing Heydrich. The operation was codenamed 'Daybreak'. Heydrich despised the Czechs, and was reckless about his personal safety. This played into the hands of the assassins. As Heydrich's driver stopped at a junction in a Prague suburb in May 1942 a gunman appeared. But his sub-machine jammed. He ran off pursued by the driver. The second assassin threw a grenade at Heydrich. He blazed away at the man, who jumped on a tram moving up the hill. It was, as one historian has noted, like a scene from the Wild West.

> **The events of 'Operation Daybreak' are well shown in the 1975 feature film of the same name starring Anthony Andrews, Martin Shaw and Tim Bottoms.**

The Germans had no penicillin and Heydrich's wounds became life threatening. But Hitler insisted on sending his personal physician to Prague. The delay was fatal and 'the Butcher of Prague' died some days later.

> **Thank God that bastard is dead.**
>
> *SS General Sepp Dietrich on hearing of Heydrich's death.*

Heinrich Himmler may have been secretly relieved that Heydrich was dead. But the SS took a terrible revenge for Heydrich's assassination. The village of Lidice outside Prague was blown up. All the men were shot, and all the women and children sent to concentration camps. Nazi claims that the people were involved in Heydrich's killing were false.

> **You can visit the ruins of Lidice today. With typical callousness the Nazis filmed the destruction of the village and the film can be seen in the museum. The new village has been deliberately rebuilt on the other side of the road.**

We can only guess about the influence Heydrich might have had if he had survived. He deserved to end up as a war criminal at Nuremburg.

THE GESTAPO

The most notorious secret police service in Germany, was also the oldest. The Geheime Staats Politzei (Secret State Police) was started by Goering in Prussia. The first letters were used to form the abbreviated Ge/sta/po. Like its successor the SD, the Gestapo had the job of destroying all opposition to Hitler in Germany. It played a big part for example in trying to track down the bomb plotters of 1944 (see Chapter 6). In fact the attempt to blow Hitler up was brought forward because the Gestapo had already arrested some conspirators. Throughout occupied Europe the Gestapo also became notorious for its tortures and murder. The men in raincoats and felt hats were feared and loathed everywhere. So was their ability to torture confessions out of people. One one occasion the Allies sent a flight of Mosquito aircraft to destroy the Gestapo headquarters in Copenhagen. This was to stop some Danish resistance fighters being tortured. The plan worked.

SS leader, Heinrich Himmler, is welcomed by Hitler.

Now listen in case you should find yourself someday in the hands of traitors or the Gestapo . . . The only change that has actually taken place consists in the fact that they are now physically your masters. Otherwise they are the same dregs of humanity that they were before you were captured.

Letter by resister Kim Malthe-Brunn smuggled out of prison January 1945

Reinhard Heydrich, Himmler's deputy, later assassinated by the Czech resistance in Prague.

THE ABWEHR

The odd man out in the Nazi security apparatus was the Abwehr, or military intelligence, which was attached to the Army. Run by Admiral Wilhelm Canaris (nicknamed 'the little admiral') it was the hiding place for many anti-Nazis, although it also did much spying work in World War Two. But the Abwehr also passed on all kind of anti-Hitler tips to the Allies. Warnings were passed on about Hitler's attack on Western Europe in 1940, and members of the Abwehr were involved in plots against him. There was a feud with the SS, and especially Heydrich, who suspected what the Abwehr was up to. In the end Canaris himself was arrested by the Gestapo and executed at Flössenburg Concentration Camp in 1945.

THE MEDIA AND THE ARTS

Paul Josef Goebbels was the most intelligent of the Nazi leaders, who believed like his boss in the value of propaganda. Originally an opponent of Hitler inside the Nazi party, Goebbels became one of his most devoted admirers. Like his master the new 'Minister of Propaganda and Enlightenment' was prepared to do anything to control the minds of the German nation, and particularly its youth.

> **If you are going to lie, lie big.**
>
> *Hitler, Mein Kampf*

Goebbels showed his awareness of the value of propaganda in Hitler's election campaigns when (with money from big business) he had thousands of small gramophones mass produced, so that supporters could play records of Hitler's speeches. Another example of this sophistication was 'Hitler Over Germany', the series of flights by the Nazi leader over Germany, between its leading cities. By contrast, British prime minister Neville Chamberlain flew in an aeroplane for the first time at the age of sixty nine, in 1938.

THE BURNING OF THE BOOKS

Nazi propaganda was essentially anti-cultural and anti-civilization. This became clear in 1933 when Goebbels organized a burning of books by authors the Nazis didn't like. They included not only Jews like Einstein, but also contemporary American writers like Ernest Hemingway. As the writer Heine observed, 'when people burn books, they soon end up burning people'.

> **When I hear the word culture, I reach for my gun.**
>
> *Hermann Goering*

What followed was the systematic brainwashing of the entire German people. On the Führer's birthday (20 April) all loyal Germans were ordered by Goebbels to hang swastika flags out of their windows. Woe betide those who did not! *Mein Kampf*, a turgid and boring work, became required reading for all Nazi party members. In it were all their Führer's wild and ill-informed ideas about art, music and literature. Having failed as a young man to get into the art academy in Vienna, Hitler was now in a position to impose his half-baked theories on all Germans. Helped by his friend and architect, Albert Speer, Hitler proceeded to cover Germany with tasteless copies of Graeco-Roman architecture. But Hitler took his building plans very seriously. When a cabaret artist, Werner Fink, poked fun at Nazi architecture, he was sent to a concentration camp.

'Subversive' books being burnt by the Nazis in Berlin in May 1933.

> **Nowadays, when I leaf through the numerous photos of models of our one-time grand boulevard, I see that it would have turned out not only crazy, but also boring.**
>
> *Albert Speer, Inside the Third Reich, 1970*

Even Hitler's deputy Rudolf Hess, responsible for one horrible red staircase, was declared 'totally unartistic' by the Führer, and forbidden to have anything to do with building anything else.

THE CINEMA

Both Hitler and Goebbels were big fans of the cinema. We know that they enjoyed private showings of Hollywood movies like *Gone With the Wind*, and the British film *Lives of A Bengal Lancer*. Hitler's favourite actress was Greta Garbo. Similar privileges were not however granted to the German people, who had to put up with many boring, tasteless movies. Film also had a clear political purpose from the earliest days of the Nazi party.

Thus the martyred Horst Wessel, in reality a bully and thug, became a Nazi hero figure on film, and had a notorious song written about him. (Wessel died in a brawl with communists.) Unpleasant anti-Jewish films portrayed them as sewer rats, and highlighted (alleged) features like long noses and sinister looks. Enemies of National Socialism were therefore cunningly stereotyped by film and radio alike.

The other kind of Nazi film was of the heroic variety. Good examples can be found in the work of Leni Riefenstähl in films like 'Triumph of the Will' (1934) and 'Olympiad' (1936). The former is a pure propaganda film of the 1934 Nazi Party Rally and starts with Hitler descending 'godlike' from the clouds. The second deals with the 1936 Berlin Olympics and covers the events well (although

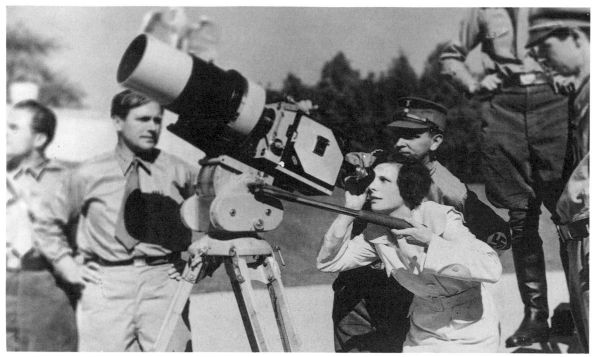

Leni Riefenstahl working on Triumph of the Will.

Hitler was furious when the black athlete Jesse Owens won four gold medals). But it starts with a dreamlike sequence where Germanic looking supermen throw javelins and discuses. All tuning in with Hitler's theories about the superiority of Germans over other races.

> **Both films can be viewed at the Imperial War Museum, London, or loaned from its film section. The sequence showing Owens winning his medals can also be seen in Programme 3 of the recent BBC World History series for schools.**

The Nazis also experimented with colour. There are some surviving colour 'home movies' which show Hitler and his friends cavorting at his mountain house. At the end of World War Two Goebbels commissioned *Kohlberg*, a heroic (and very costly) work about the Napoleonic Wars. Although tedious to watch, it was technically advanced for its day, and in full colour.

RADIO

Goebbels was an excellent broadcaster and public speaker. He was the only Nazi leader, according to Hitler, whose speeches didn't send him to sleep. This talent was put to full use by the man his enemies called 'the poisoned dwarf' (Goebbels was very small and had a club foot which never appeared in Nazi propaganda films). He was also nicknamed 'the father of lies'.

It was Goebbels who made key speeches during the war, and went on the radio in 1944 to reassure the German people after opposition generals tried to blow Hitler up.

Josef Goebbels, Nazi Minister of Propaganda. He was an excellent broadcaster and public speaker.

Do you want total war? Do you reject the Jewish-Bolshevik demand for unconditional surrender? Do you accept that anyone who detracts from the war effort will lose his head? Long live Germany.

Part of Goebbels' 1943 speech rejecting the Allied demand for unconditional surrender.

But some of his 'black propaganda' during World War Two was very effective too. In France in 1940 the Germans were skilful in telling Frenchmen that their British allies were leaving them to do all the fighting. Stories were spread about new German secret weapons and nuns with hobnailed boots who were meant to be German spies behind the lines! Goebbels used the traitor William Joyce (nicknamed 'Lord Haw Haw') to broadcast directly to wartime Britain. Sometimes his knowledge of troop movements frightened people, but more often his rather wild stories—always starting 'Germany calling, Germany calling' in his super-posh voice—were better listening than the BBC.

Goebbels' more important task was to reinforce the iron grip of the Nazi Party on the lives of ordinary German people. They had little idea of what was really going on during the war (Stalingrad was effectively presented as a victory rather than a defeat), and were bombarded with a ceaseless flow of official lies—Churchill was a drunken warmonger, and Roosevelt a 'Jew-Bolshevik' while all the peoples of Occupied Europe were supposed to love Hitler's 'New Order'.

The biggest lie of all was saved for the end. Battered, and bewildered Germany was told on German radio in April 1945 that its beloved Führer had died fighting at the head of his troops. In reality both Hitler and Goebbels had committed suicide.

THE PRESS

Hitler, unlike his fellow dictator Benito Mussolini, had not been a journalist, but he had a keen awareness of the power of the press. One of Hitler's right-wing rivals before 1933 was Alfred Hugenburg, and he owned a chain of newspapers. So one of the Nazi government's earliest moves was to ban all anti-Nazi newspapers, although it couldn't prevent the circulation of underground pamphlets.

> **According to the American journalist William L. Shirer (author of *The Rise and Fall of the Third Reich* which is well worth reading; Pan Books), the effect of Nazi propaganda was 'to afflict the German people with radio programmes and motion pictures as inane and boring as were the contents of daily newspapers and periodicals'.**

Julius Streicher, editor of the anti-Semitic newspaper 'Der Stürmer', a satirical montage by the anti-Nazi artist John Heartfield.

Most Nazi newspapers were embarrassingly bad, if not actually obscene. The arch anti-Semite journalist Julius Streicher, generally seen with a rawhide whip in his hand, had to be quietly exiled to the countryside. He founded *Der Stürmer* ('The Stormer') newspaper in 1922. His frenzied newspaper attacks on Jews set the pattern for the Nazi press. Goebbels himself started *Der Angriff* (The Assault) which was so bad that he called it 'Baloney in print', and it had to be remodelled (ironically) on the party newspaper of the Nazis' hated enemies, the communists. 'The Assault' appeared before 1933, and eventually became the accepted Nazi party paper, but the *Völkischer Beobachter* ('The Racist Observer') started right back in 1920. One of its first headlines was 'Do a Real Job on the Jews'! All these newspapers (if we can flatter them with such a name) also attacked Weimar politicians, Versailles, and the communists in the years of opposition. After 1933 they helped form part of the Nazi media front.

> **His speech was glutted with sadistic imagery and he relished attacking personal enemies in the foulest terms. Convinced that the Jew was plotting against the Aryan world, he had an endless catalogue of abuse at the tip of his tongue.**
>
> *John Toland's description of Streicher*

Hitler and Goebbels at the Nazi-organized exhibition of 'degenerate' art.

It is significant that at the Nazi War Crimes Tribunal at Nuremberg in 1946 the Allied judges thought Streicher's propaganda so foul that they had him hanged. Yet Streicher didn't fight in the war, and there was no evidence that he had killed anybody. Goebbels escaped the hangman by killing himself, and the Allies tried his subordinate Hans Fritsche. But there was no real evidence against him, and he was acquitted.

MUSIC AND OPERA

It may seem impossible for a government to interfere with music but the Nazis managed it. On the one hand they loved Wagner, whose operas in the *Ring* cycle were full of flaxen-haired German warrior maidens. Hitler was a great friend of Wagner's daughter-in-law, Frau Winnifred Wagner (an English-woman by birth) and spent a lot of time at the annual festival of Wagner's music at Bay-reuth. But Jewish composers like Felix Men-delssohn had their work banned. Unfortu-nately this Nazi campaign was given some

respectability by world-famous musicians like Richard Strauss, who co-operated with them.

At the other end of the scale the Nazis made effective use of popular songs like the 'Horst Wessel Lied' and (in the war) 'Lili Marlene'. The latter actually became as popu-lar with the British in the Western Desert campaign as it did with the Germans.

Abstract art was banned, and replaced by paintings of muscular supermen and blonde maidens. The Führer had fancied himself as an artist in his youth in Vienna. But all his little landscapes on postcards (sold for him extraordinarily enough by a Jewish partner in Vienna) mysteriously disappeared from circu-lation after 1933! The Führer of Germany could not be known as a postcard painter. British propaganda in World War Two about Hitler being a 'house painter', although amus-ing, was in fact false. But he did have a cousin called William Patrick Hitler who lived in Liverpool!

Everyone uses propaganda, especially in wartime, when the need to win makes people 'economical with the truth'. But Nazi propaganda was based on a philosophy of lies, so that it didn't matter whether it was wartime or peacetime. Central to it was the lie that Germans were superior to other races, and could ill-treat or kill them as they pleased. There is a clear difference between using every available technical trick to prove the rightness of a cause, and telling your citizens that others are sub-human and unfit to live. Whether such outrageous propaganda deserves a death sentence, as in the case of Streicher, is an open question. But in Britain today we have laws against incitement to racial hatred and the wearing of Nazi-style uniforms. This is one result of Nazi hate propaganda between 1933 and 1945.

THE JEWISH QUESTION

Adolf Hitler's fanatical hatred of the Jews is very difficult to understand. There is no evidence that he had anything to do with Jews in his youth (apart from the episode mentioned on page 32). But by the time Hitler joined the German army in 1914 he had become rabidly anti-Jewish.

> **Wherever I went I began to see Jews, the more I saw, the more sharply they became distinguished in my eyes, from the rest of humanity.**
>
> *Hitler, Mein Kampf*

The answer seems to lie with the period Hitler spent as a failed artist in Vienna between 1909 and 1913 (when he went to Munich). Vienna had a long tradition of anti-Semitism, and had some very unpleasant anti-Jewish newspapers, which Hitler undoubtedly read. The basis for Hitler's anti-Semitism seems to have been *jealousy*. Jews were successful in Vienna. They were important figures in business, the arts and banking (e.g. the Rothschilds). Hitler already had an inferiority complex because he failed to pass his school certificate, and couldn't get into the art and architectural academies. Surviving records show this failure. For Hitler then anti-Semitism seems to have been the politics of envy. Plenty of others shared his opinion.

A crude and primitive philosophy de-veloped from this jealousy. Jews seduced innocent German (or Aryan) women. They were grasping financiers. Later they helped with their Bolshevik allies to bring Germany down to defeat in 1918. (Like most half truths there was something in this. Bolsheviks [communists as we would call them today] like Trotsky and Zinoviev were Jews.)

Worst of all, the Jews were polluting the pure blood of the German master race. All these mad ideas were put into Hitler's book *Mein Kampf* which he wrote when he was in prison in 1924. Jews were 'sub-human' (untermenschen) and they and their influence in Europe had to be destroyed. Europe, according to the half-educated Hitler (who always sneered at 'professors' and fully-educated people) lay at the mercy of an imagined 'Jewish-Bolshevik conspiracy'.

> **The sun will not shine again for the people of the earth until the last Jew has died.**
>
> *Julius Streicher*

Once in power in 1933, Hitler was in a position to unleash his hatred of the Jews. A programme of 'creeping anti-Semitism' was started. First of all their businesses were boycotted, and Jews were beaten up in the streets by SA men. Then they were excluded from the professions like medicine, the law

34

nd teaching. Then in 1935 the Nazis intro-
duced anti-Jewish laws.

> **1. Only a national of German or similar blood is a citizen of the Reich. A Jew is not a citizen of the Reich. He has no vote. He may not fill public office.**
> **2. Marriage between Jews and nationals of German blood is forbidden.**
>
> *Extract from the 1935 Nuremberg laws*

These laws, named after the city of Nuremberg where the Nazi party held its annual
ally, deprived Jews of their citizenship. They
therefore became *stateless*, and had to wear
he Star of David as a symbol of identity. No
ew was allowed to have a German woman
ervant under 35 years of age.

Briefly in 1936, the anti-Jewish campaign
was toned down. This was because Germany
was acting as host for the Olympic Games.
Hitler didn't want the more disgusting as-
pects of Nazi Germany on full view to
foreigners. Not, of course, that any Jews were
llowed to compete in the German team.

> **You can still visit the stadium built for the 1936 Olympic Games, in Berlin. It is one of the less tasteless examples of Nazi architecture.**

Even so, the Nazis bent the rules when it
uited them. Goering, for example, kept on
ome specially gifted Jewish airmen in the
uftwaffe. There were even rumours that
itler and Heydrich (Himmler's sinister
eputy) had Jewish ancestry.

HE CRYSTAL NIGHT

Once all the foreigners were safely out of

Germany, the anti-Jewish campaign started
up again. Tragically, many Jewish families
didn't read the warning signs and get out
while there was still time. This would have
meant losing all their property to the Nazi
government, and many Jews had been in
Germany for centuries. Others thought that
Hitler was a sort of 'historical freak'. Germany was supposed, after all, to be a civilized
country, which had produced composers like
Handel and writers like Goethe and Schiller.
Things would soon return to normal.

Any such dreams were shattered in
November 1938. This was during the so-
called 'Crystal Night' (Kristallnacht in German), an act of revenge by the Nazis, when a
young Jew shot dead a member of the German embassy in Paris. Ironically this man,
von Rath, was actually being watched by the
secret police, who suspected him of being
part of the underground resistance to Hitler.
Egged on by the 'Poisoned Dwarf', Doctor
Goebbels, the SA went on the rampage,
burning synagogues and Jewish businesses.
In Berlin alone 'The Night of the Crystals',
named after the shining of the broken shop
glass, cost 36 Jewish lives and resulted in the
burning of 191 synagogues. Thousands of
Jews were taken away to concentration
camps, and their property was seized by the
Nazis. They were also made to pay a huge
fine of a thousand million marks.

> **For the time being, only healthy men, not too old, are to be arrested. Upon their arrest, the appropriate concentration camps should be contacted immediately in order to confine them in these camps as fast as possible.**
>
> *Orders sent to the Security Police on 'Crystal Night', 1938*

The *New York Times'* correspondent reported that the 'wave of destruction' was 'unparalleled in Germany', and you may wonder how foreign countries reacted. Generally the Jewish issue was regarded as a German domestic matter. US President Roosevelt said that he 'could scarcely believe that such things could happen in the twentieth century'. Such remarks would have been more impressive had the USA (and Britain and France) had a better record for taking desperate Jewish refugees. It was easy enough to receive, and use the talents of, the great Jewish mathematician Albert Einstein. But many other Jews were turned away and perished in Hitler's death camps.

THE FINAL SOLUTION

The campaign against the Jews reached new, and more hideous heights, as the tentacles of Hitler's 'Third Reich' reached out into the rest of Europe. Every country that fell under the swastika had its anti-Jewish terror. But each reacted differently. In France the fascist style 'Milice' (police) actively helped to round up French Jews and send them to their deaths. In Denmark, by contrast, heroic efforts were made to smuggle Jews away to neutral Sweden. On one notable occasion the whole of Copenhagen staged a one-day protest against Nazi barbarism. In another case, the family of the present Israeli prime minister Shamir was betrayed to the Nazis by a (so-called) Catholic Polish farmer. The picture was a patchy one, but there were individual acts of tremendous heroism. Perhaps the most celebrated was the saving of many thousands of Hungarian Jews by the Swedish diplomat Raoul Wallenburg who gave them all Swedish passports. The scale of Jewish suffering is indicated in the following table.

Number of Jewish Deaths By Country 1933–45	
Poland	2,600,000
USSR	750,000
Hungary	700,000
Rumania	500,000
Germany	180,000
Netherlands	104,000
Lithuania	104,000
France	65,000
Austria	60,000
Czechoslovakia	60,000

Initially this horror was somewhat haphazard. Jewish men, women and children were shot in the back of the head, and pushed into open trenches. Then execution method became more systematic.

We know about the origins of the so-called 'Final Solution'. On 20 January 1942 an important meeting was held at Wannsee on the outskirts of Berlin. Present were Reinhard Heydrich, Himmler's deputy, Gestapo chief Müller, and SS Lieutenant Colonel Adolf Eichmann, together with other members of the Nazi government. During the conference Heydrich told his colleagues that he had been given 'the responsibility for working out *the final solution* of the Jewish problem'. This solution was horrific in its simplicity. Physically fit Jews would be worked to death in labour gangs. Unfit Jews would be killed (the means weren't spelt out at Wannsee).

> When one pulls out a tooth, one does it with a single tug, and the pain quickly goes. The Jew must clear out of Europe. It's the Jew who prevents everything. When I think about it I realize that I'm extraordinarily humane.
>
> *Adolf Hitler, 23 January 1942*

It is said that after Heydrich and Eichmann had discussed the mass murder of the Jews, they jumped on to a table and drank a toast. It was a guilt which Hans Frank, another Nazi, said would be with the German people for a thousand years.

THE DEATH CAMPS

The decision made, the means of mass murder were easily found. It involved what British prime minister Churchill called 'perverted science', and the use of the whole of German industry. The most efficient way of disposing of unwanted Jews was to gas them. Gas ovens and Xylon B gas were provided (with invoices) by 'respectable' firms like Siemens and I. G. Farben. Millions were to die in Auschwitz, Buchenwald, Treblinka, Belsen and a score of others. Hitler's insane fantasies were made real.

> **It is possible to visit the former camp at Buchenwald in Eastern Germany. It is in the woods just outside the old historic town of Weimar, where the Republican constitution was drawn up in 1919. There you can see for yourself the ovens, the clothing of the victims, and even the railway platform where the murdered people arrived.**

Did the German people know what was happening? It is hard to believe that they did not. Trains full of wretched Jews travelled through German stations, and SS guards had families and relatives. Industrialists as indicated above supplied gas ovens and gas itself. It was easy to blame Hitler after 1945 when he was conveniently dead. The Allies made sure that in places like Belsen, the local people were *made* to see the piles of corpses and their leftovers, and to smell the stench of

death. When SS camp commanders said they were 'only obeying orders' this defence wasn't accepted.

> **There is much footage on the concentration camps. Some in old Pathé newsreel, others like the unusual (and disturbing) colour film in the American 'From D Day To Berlin' TV reconstructions can never really convey the horror of the camps, although some like 'Escape from Sobibor' make an effort to do so.**

THE JEWISH RESISTANCE

One of the things that has puzzled people about the 'Final Solution', or the 'Holocaust' as it is often known, is why the Jews didn't resist. Many thousands of people apparently allowed themselves to be murdered without resistance, by the Nazis. Several points need to be remembered here. Many Jewish communities in Germany and elsewhere had long experience of persecution (Christian Europe blamed Jews for the crucifixion and death of Jesus Christ). Their leaders therefore believed that it was best to keep a 'low profile'. This often meant doing what the Nazis said.

There was also an element of trickery. Jews were shipped off to death camps believing that they would be put to work for the Reich. When they arrived at their destination they were told to undress for 'delousing'. They were then pushed into a chamber into which crystals of Xylon B gas were pumped. Imagine the horror of people of both sexes and all ages herded together gasping desperately for air. The dead were often found (according to eyewitnesses) in the shape of a pyramid. The strongest and most desperate were at the top near the air vents. Small wonder that camp inmates talked of the 'death of God'.

It is often forgotten that there *was* a Jewish resistance. There were revolts at Treblinka and Sobibor, where 300 Jews escaped in October 1943. Much larger in scale was the uprising in the Warsaw Ghetto (also in 1943), the area of the city into which the Jews were herded. Over-crowding and disease gave the Jews in the ghetto desperate courage, and they got some help from the Polish Resistance. The resisters took refuge in the sewers and surprised even the Nazis by their bravery. The whole ghetto was destroyed and its defenders butchered. But the heroes of the Warsaw Ghetto are remembered today in Israel and throughout the Jewish world.

> **With their bones broken, they still tried to crawl across the street into buildings which had not yet been set on fire ... Despite the danger of being burned alive the Jews and bandits often preferred to return into the flames rather than risk being caught by us.**
>
> SS General Jürgen Stroop reporting on the Warsaw Ghetto uprising, May 1943.

According to Nazi racial theories such Jewish resistance, from inferior types, was impossible. But some survivors of the Holocaust actually survived to see justice done. Adolf Eichmann was seized by Israeli secret agents in 1961 in Argentina, and taken to the new Jewish state for punishment. After a long trial in the full glare of publicity, he was found guilty and executed. Currently the trial of 'Ivan the Terrible' concerns the atrocities committed by a Ukrainian SS guard at Treblinka. The SS murderer Klaus Barbie was serving life imprisonment in France until his death in 1991.

THE NUREMBERG TRIALS

More systematic justice was dealt out by the Allies in 1946. Fittingly, these war crimes trials were held at Nuremberg, where the infamous laws of 1935 were announced. One of the major charges against the Nazi leaders was 'crimes against humanity' of which the most serious was genocide. *Genocide* means the murder of a race, and the Nazis had tried to murder the whole Jewish race. An eternal flame burns in memory of those six million victims in the Israeli capital today.

The Holocaust is the biggest horror in a century of horrors. It still casts its shadow over the modern world. Without Nazi barbarism there would have been no Jewish state today. Without Israel there would be no Palestinian refugee camps today. The people of the Gaza Strip are in a sense Hitler's victims.

> **I twist my heart round again, so that the bad is on the outside and the good is on the inside, and keep on trying to find a way of becoming what I would so like to be and what I could be, if ... there weren't any other people living in the world.**
>
> Yours Ann

This is the last entry in *The Diary of Ann Frank*, a Jewish girl who died in Belsen from typhus just three months before her sixteenth birthday. She had been hiding from the Nazis in the attic of a house in Amsterdam for two years.

Ann Frank's house survives today in Amsterdam and you can see where she and her family hid from the Gestapo. Her diary, which is published in paperback, is well worth reading, and her story has been made into a feature film.

THE ROAD TO THE FINAL SOLUTION

1924 Publication of Hitler's *Mein Kampf* (My Struggle).

1933 Hitler becomes Chancellor. Start of Jewish Persecution.

1935 Nuremberg Laws.

1936 Berlin Olympics.

1938 Crystal Night.

1939 Start of World War Two.

1942 Wannsee Conference decides on 'Final Solution'. Death camps begin operating.

1943 Uprising in Warsaw Ghetto.

1945 Death of Ann Frank in Belsen. End of World War Two. Camps liberated.

GERMANS AGAINST HITLER

It is easy to believe that all Germans were enthusiastic Nazis. But this was not the case. While National Socialism was a popular movement, it is important to remember that Hitler never got a majority in a free election. In the last free election in March 1933, the Nazis (despite all their propaganda) only got 43 per cent of the vote. After 1933 Hitler got enormous majorities in plebiscites, but it was assumed that everyone had voted yes. To vote no, risked identification by the Nazis and needed considerable courage.

RESIDENTS OF NORTHEIM!
You want to continue your work in peace and quiet! You've had enough of the impudent behaviour of the SPD and KPD! You want the red Senators, Councilmen, and Reichbanner* Generals with all their armed followers to go to the Devil!

Typical Nazi anti-socialist and anti-communist propaganda in the March 1933 elections.
Source: The Nazi Seizure of Power, William Sheridan Allen, 1965

The terror system described in Chapter 4

* Reichbanner=the Social Democrats Private Army (like the Nazi SA).

frightened most Germans into accepting National Socialism. Only a heroic minority actively opposed the Nazis. Some were communists (their leader Ernst Thälmann died in Buchenwald concentration camp). Others were conservatives and army officers. Still more were churchmen and students. This chapter tells their story.

THE PROBLEM OF REMOVING HITLER

Even though Hitler was such an evil dictator, opinions were divided about how to get rid of him. In the late 1930s a group of army officers formed around General Ludwig Beck for this purpose. But these soldiers had a special problem in dealing with Hitler. Back in 1933 they had taken a personal oath of loyalty to the Führer. Could they now break this sacred oath? Some felt that to arrest Hitler was alright, but to kill him was not. In 1938 the military plotters hoped that the West would do the job for them by fighting Hitler over the Sudetenland. They were sure he would lose and could then be arrested. Unfortunately Britain and France failed to oblige. The plotters did nothing.

ELSER'S PLOT

The boldest move against Hitler was made by an ordinary worker. Georg Elser was a cabinet maker, who hated Nazism, and worked entirely alone. He didn't belong to any political party.

In November 1939 Hitler made his usual visit to Munich on the anniversary of the failed beerhall putsch of 1923. He went to the beer-cellar where the failed uprising had been started when he, Hitler, had fired a pistol into the ceiling. For some reason Hitler left a little early. Moments later, the bomb which Elser had cleverly hidden in a pillar exploded. Elser was arrested and executed. Not for the first time Hitler was saved by some primitive instinct for danger. Like many evil tyrants, he seemed to have nine lives.

> Hitler's greatest bloodless victory had removed . . . temporarily the possibility of arresting him as plainly a madman who would plunge Germany into war and restored his reputation as a wonder-worker. There were also immense practical difficulties. The generals could not control where they might be posted or when they might be replaced. As neither telephone calls nor written messages were safe in Nazi Germany, personal visits had to be made to prepare any clandestine plans; nothing on a large scale could be improvised suddenly.
>
> *David Astor, The Challenge of The Third Reich, 1986*

The Munich beerhall after Georg Elser's failed attempt on Hitler's life in 1939.

After this Hitler drove about in a bullet proof Mercedes car, with toughened steel armourplating, and a laminated glass windshield.

> **The news made a vivid impression on Hitler. He fell very silent, and then described it as a miracle that the bomb missed him.**
>
> *Hitler's Air Force aide von Below describes his reaction to Elser's attempt on his life in 1939.*

THE WHITE ROSE

Even open non-violent opposition to Nazism was very dangerous in Germany. This was proved in the case of the Weisse Rose (White Rose) organization in Munich. This group of teachers and students was responsible for dropping anti-Nazi leaflets into the main lobby of Munich University in February 1943. The student leaders (ranging from just 22 to 25 years of age) were all beheaded, a typical piece of Nazi savagery. The intention was obviously to terrorize ordinary people.

> **I never knew that dying is so easy . . . I die without any feeling of hatred . . . Never forget that life is nothing but a growing in love and a preparation for eternity.**
>
> *Christopher Probst, White Rose member, to his sister before execution, 1943.*

THE BACKGROUND TO THE 1944 BOMB PLOT

Meantime the attempts to assassinate Hitler by officers and members of the Abwehr (military intelligence) went on. The dictator continued to enjoy amazing good luck. In one case in 1943 a British made bomb was successfully smuggled on to Hitler's personal aircraft. The conspirators waited confidently for news of Hitler's death. It never came. It turned out that the cold on the Eastern Front, where the bomb parts had been kept, had corroded the mechanism. Fortunately one of the conspirators managed to get the bomb back without anything being suspected. He took the bomb to pieces again on the train back to Berlin!

On another occasion an officer volunteered to model a new uniform before Hitler. He would have two hand grenades in the jacket pockets, enough to blow him and the Führer up. Hitler cancelled the show at the last moment.

THE CHURCHMEN

From the early days some Christian clergy like Pastor Neimöller had been openly critical of Nazism. But like Beck and the officers they too had a problem. Was it moral for Christians to kill a man, even one as evil as Hitler? By 1943 some clergymen like the Protestant Dietrich Bonhoeffer decided that it was. He became actively involved in the bomb plot to kill Hitler.

In the event the Gestapo put Bonhoeffer in prison in 1943. But he kept quiet about what he knew of the plot.

> **If we claim to be Christians there is no room for expediency. Hitler is Antichrist; therefore we must go on with our work and eliminate him, whether he be successful or not.**
>
> *Dietrich Bonhoeffer, 1943*

The key plotter was Count Claus von Stauffenburg, a war hero. As a man who had lost one eye, an arm, and three fingers from

Dietrich Bonhoeffer, Protestant clergyman and conspirator against Hitler.

like Adam von Trott zu Solz also supported the plotters.

20 JULY 1944

The plan was simple. As a staff, or planning officer, Stauffenburg had access to Hitler's headquarters at Rastenburg in East Prussia. On 20 July 1944 he was invited to a conference there to be attended by Hitler and other leading figures. Stauffenburg would take a briefcase into the Conference. The conspirators expected that the terribly wounded Stauffenburg wouldn't be properly searched before he went into the wooden conference hut. They were right. Again the bomb was of British make, consisting of a slab of plastic high explosive. At a pre-arranged moment Stauffenburg would get a telephone call. He would leave his briefcase under the conference table. At 12.37 the call came and Claus von Stauffenburg left the room. At 12.42 the bomb went off, blowing the wooden hut apart. Stauffenburg didn't believe that Hitler could possibly have survived. He got through the camp gates before anyone realized what was happening. Another conspirator sabotaged the Rastenburg telephone lines.

the other hand in North Africa he was unlikely to arouse Nazi suspicions. So this made him a perfect leader for the bomb conspiracy. He led those younger officers who were angered by Beck's dithering (although he did agree to be in a new government). Stauffenburg's conspirators also won over Field Marshal Erwin Rommel, the hero of the desert war against the British. By 1944 Rommel, a non political professional soldier, realized Hitler was leading Germany to disaster. Unfortunately for the conspirators, Rommel's car was dive bombed by an RAF fighter sometime before the attempt on Hitler's life. When it took place he was still recovering from his wounds. But the conspiracy had a lot of support from anti-Nazi officers in Berlin and occupied Paris. Foreign Office members

> **The building was wrecked and a great hole blown in the floor. But the oaken support and the table top had saved Hitler ... His right arm had been so badly bruised as to be temporarily paralysed, he was deafened, in his right ear permanently, his right trouser leg had been torn off and both legs were burned as was his hair, while a falling beam had caught his back.**
>
> *Constantine FitzGibbon, The Shirt of Nessus, 1964*

Hitler holding his damaged arm in the aftermath of the July bomb plot.

In fact Hitler did survive largely because he was leaning over the wooden table when the bomb went off. The officer next to Stauffenburg had also pushed the briefcase near a wooden support after he had left the room. Both these factors lessened the effect of the blast.

> ### If only the swine were dead.
> *Field Marshal von Kluge, 20 July 1944.*

Even so the plot might have succeeded if the conspirators had acted decisively. They did so in Paris. But in Berlin there were mistakes, and the conspirators crucially failed to arrest Goebbels. The cunning propaganda minister rallied support, and got the shaken Führer to broadcast to the German people. Once it was known that Hitler was still alive some of the conspirators, including Stauffenburg and Beck (who botched a suicide attempt) were shot by firing squad. They were to be the lucky ones.

> ### A very small clique of ambitious officers, devoid of conscience and at the same time criminally stupid, had forged a conspiracy to remove me . . .
> *Adolf Hitler in a broadcast on 21 July 1944.*

Hitler's revenge was to be terrible indeed. Anyone remotely linked to the bomb plot was arrested. Their families were sent to concentration camps. At the trial the conspirators were even deprived of belts, so that they were humiliated by having to hold up their trousers.

Hitler's bullying prosecutor Roland Freisler, who had studied Stalin's show trials, presided (it was some justice that he later died in an Allied air raid). He shouted abuse at the defendants. All the surviving leaders were sentenced to death. To make their end especially painful, they were hanged slowly with piano wire. Hitler had a film made of the

Adam von Trott zu Solz on trial for his part in the conspiracy to kill Hitler.

Erwin Rommel with Hitler. Implicated in the conspiracy to kill Hitler he was forced to commit suicide.

executions. He made army officers watch it as a warning.

As many as 4000 people may have died in the bloodbath after the bomb plot. Many Germans regarded Stauffenburg, von Trott, and their friends as traitors. But some historians feel that they didn't get enough encouragement from the Allies.

Nazi hypocrisy was shown by the fate of Rommel. It was very embarrassing for the Nazis to have to put their most famous general on trial. So they gave him a choice. Trial and concentration camp for Rommel's family. Or Rommel's suicide, a hero's funeral and his family's safety. Rommel shot himself.

> **The failure of the July plot was the fault of the Resisters themselves. They would have been the first to say—had they lived—that it was a German affair and that the Germans should take the credit or the blame for success or failure.**
>
> *Giles MacDonagh, A Good German: Adam von Trott zu Solz, 1989.*

> **The atmosphere of the time is well conveyed by the film *Rommel: The Desert Fox.***
>
> *Made by Hollywood in 1951 and starring James Mason.*

THE ROAD TO WAR 1933-9

HITLER'S PLAN

In his book *Mein Kampf* (My Struggle) written in prison in 1924, Adolf Hitler laid down a sort of blueprint for Nazi foreign policy. In it he made clear his hatred of the Versailles Treaty, which defeated Germany had been made to sign in 1919.

When he came to power Hitler said he would tear up this 'diktat' (the German word for a dictated settlement). Only when this had been done could Hitler move on to stage two of his plan, the making of a German Empire or Reich.

> **Peace treaties whose demands are a scourge to nations not seldom strike the first roll for the uprising to come.**
>
> *Adolf Hitler, Mein Kampf*

This was because according to Hitler 'When the territory of the Reich embraces all Germans, only then can the right arise, from the need of the people, to acquire foreign territory.' If you study the map on page 59, you can see the areas where these homeless Germans lived—Germans Hitler was determined to bring inside his new German Empire. Later he was forced to make one or

two exceptions, but in 1924 all that lay far off in the future.

Hitler used a special word for the 'foreign territory' which Germany would need. This was *lebensraum* or 'living space' (a more popular translation would be elbow room). This would be found in the East in Russia or Poland. If the Poles and Russians objected it didn't matter. They were sub human (*untermenschen*) Slavs who would be used as slave labour in Hitler's new 'Thousand Year Reich' (it actually lasted 12 years). Don't confuse 'Slavs' with 'slaves'! Slavs are a racial grouping (Russians, Poles, Czechs, Bulgars) who live in Eastern Europe to this day.

> **When we think of a new territory in Europe today, we must principally think of Russia and the border states subject to her.**
>
> *Adolf Hitler, Mein Kampf*

Only after the Nazis came to power in 1933 was Hitler in a position to carry out his ambitious and insane plans. Even then he had to 'box cleverly' for a couple of years. The other European powers were suspicious of Nazi intentions, although some foreign leaders hadn't bothered to read *Mein Kampf*.

In order to promote his territorial ambitions Hitler created an enormously powerful military machine.

I have the impression that the persons directing the policy of the Hitler government are not normal. Many of us indeed, have a feeling that we are living in a country where fantastic hooligans and eccentrics have got the upper hand.

British Ambassador Rumbold reporting to London in 1933.

YEARS OF WAITING

Hitler knew he would have to move carefully. Although he took Germany out of the League of Nations in 1933, he balanced this by making a non-aggression pact with Poland in 1934. This, of course, was a clever ploy by Hitler because everyone knew how much Germans resented the loss of the so-called 'Polish Corridor' (refer to page 59).

But in that same year 1934 Hitler was also reminded of the need for caution, when a crisis arose over his homeland Austria. There was an Austrian Nazi party and it was naturally encouraged when Hitler came to power. In July 1934 Austrian Nazis tried to seize power, and one of them shot the Austrian Chancellor Englebert Dollfuss in his office. Dollfuss was left to bleed to death on the carpet.

Whether Hitler actually knew about what the Austrian Nazis were up to is uncertain, but everyone *thought* he did. The Italian dictator Mussolini was especially angry because Doll-fuss's wife and family were staying with him at the time. He regarded Austria as a special area of Italian interest, and rushed troops up to the Italian-Austrian border. Germany was 'warned off' and Hitler had to hand over Dollfuss's murderers, who had fled to Germany. Germany was too weak to fight in 1934, but Hitler still meant to unite Austria and Germany, even though the Treaty of Versailles forbade it. The events of 1934 showed that Hitler could put aside his long term plans (as with the Polish Treaty) when he had to. Britain and France backed Italy up in a meeting at Stresa in 1935.

> **It is unlikely, in fact, that Hitler knew what was planned. This was no time for foreign adventures, so soon after the events of 30 June.**
>
> *British historian Alan Bullock on the Dollfuss murder.*

Germany was told to keep out of Austrian affairs. Then Hitler got an unexpected bonus. This was when Britain, without talking to her French ally first, made important naval concessions. Germany could build up to 35 per cent of Royal Navy strength, a clear rejection of the naval clauses of Versailles, which stopped her having a proper navy at all.

> **The happiest day of my life.**
>
> *Hitler on hearing about the Anglo-German Naval Treaty.*

This Anglo-German Naval Treaty was a valuable sign to Hitler that he could get what he wanted. Why did the British allow it? Their motives were linked to the so-called policy of 'appeasement' you will read about later in this chapter.

THE RHINELAND REOCCUPIED

Early in March 1936 Hitler pulled off the first of what became known to the press as his 'Saturday surprises'. He tended to do things at weekends so catching the British government ministers out shooting grouse, and the French in the middle of one of their many political crises!

This was the reoccupation of the Rhineland by the tiny German army which Hitler had increased to 300,000 men the previous year (so breaking the Versailles Treaty). Europe held its breath, expecting France to react. But she did not.

There were several reasons for this. Firstly, Britain wouldn't help and France wouldn't move without her. (The French remembered 1923 when they had occupied the coalmining area of the Ruhr, and had to withdraw after Britain refused to support her.) Then France had a caretaker government in place just before elections. Finally, the French Commander-in-Chief said that to deal with Germany, the whole army would have to be mobilized and this would be unpopular. So nothing happened, even though Hitler had broken the treaty of 1919 which said that Germany could have no soldiers in the demilitarized Rhineland. His generals were immensely relieved, and Hitler himself declared the Rhineland crisis as 'the most nerve wracking forty eight hours of my life'.

> **The Germans are only going into their own back garden.**
>
> *Lord Lothian, a British politician on the Rhineland crisis in 1936.*

The Führer became even more convinced of his own divine mission to save Germany, and less likely to listen to advice. By contrast France's small allies Belgium, Poland and Czechoslovakia began to wonder whether she could be relied upon. The Belgians decided that she could not, and declared themselves neutral.

Should Hitler have been stopped in 1936? Many historians used to think so, but we now know that Hitler did have plans for desperate resistance if the French had moved. In reality neither France nor Britain wanted to fight over the Rhineland, which was part of Germany anyway. But there is no doubt that the fact that Hitler had 'got away with it' was a grave danger to the peace of Europe.

> **The French ministers looked at each other in horror. Mobilization! And six weeks before an election! It was madness. The electorate would never stand for it. Parliamentary defeat would be certain—why their very jobs were at stake.**
>
> *Extract from Alistair Horne, To Lose a Battle, 1990*

THE SPANISH CIVIL WAR

Hitler's cause was also helped by the outbreak of a new crisis in 1936, which conveniently switched attention away from Central Europe. In July the Spanish army revolted against the Republican government. It was helped by the Spanish Fascist Party (Falange).

So Hitler decided to help the rebel leader General Francisco Franco, as did Mussolini.

Most of the German help was in the air. Hitler sent Luftwaffe (Air Force) pilots to Spain, where they could try out new dive bombing techniques. This Kondor Legion, as it became known, made a devastating raid on the town of Guernica in 1937. Hundreds died in the bombing.

> **The Spanier were such a close group. Whatever they decided that was it. 'Spanier' (Spaniards) was the slang for all the ex-Civil War pilots. Their successes against the Republicans in Spain meant they were already highly decorated and highly paid.**
>
> *Ulrich Steinhilperex—Messerschmitt Pilot, 1990.*

The experience gained by these pilots was to be important at the start of World War Two.

THE ROME-BERLIN AXIS

The Spanish War also brought the two fascist dictators Hitler and Mussolini closer together. This process started when Mussolini fell out with the western powers over his invasion of Abyssinia (now Ethiopia) in 1935. Its conquest was complete by the summer of 1936. Then in November 1936, the dictators became firm friends. This was through an agreement called the Rome-Berlin Axis. It wasn't a military agreement but a promise of co-operation. The military agreement came later. The Rome-Berlin Axis was obviously aimed at communist Russia. In World War Two the German-Italian alliance was referred to as the 'Axis Powers'.

Hitler with General Franco.

> **...This Berlin-Rome line is not a diaphragm but rather an axis around which can revolve all those European states with a will to collaboration and peace.**
>
> *Benito Mussolini, November 1936.*

A year later Germany and Italy were joined by Japan in an Anti-Comintern Pact. It was set up to fight world communism (*The Comintern* was the international wing of the Soviet communist party). In the meantime Mussolini had been mesmerized by a visit to Nazi Germany. 'When Fascism has a friend,' he told the German crowds, 'it will march with that friend to the last.' It is also true that Mussolini was the only friend Adolf Hitler remained loyal to in his life.

All these events are covered in Programme 3 of the recent BBC TV series on Twentieth Century World History.

APPEASEMENT

A dictionary definition of the word 'appease' is 'to pacify', perhaps by listening to your opponent's arguments. Yet 'appeasement' became a dirty word as a result of what happened in the 1930s. It was especially associated with the British Prime Minister

Neville Chamberlain (1937–40), although his predecessor Stanley Baldwin (1935–37) also followed an appeasement policy. The appeasers believed (a) that Germany had been badly treated by the Versailles Treaty and (b) Britain should make concessions to win back German friendship. Neville Chamberlain developed the appeasement policy in his own special way, through what he called his 'double line'. This meant firstly negotiating with Hitler, to see what he wanted. Secondly building up Britain's armed strength especially in the air. Everyone in the 1930s went to see films like 'The Shape of Things to Come', and were very worried by this, as well as newsreels from Spain which showed the Kondor Legion (see page 49) at work. British rearmament revolved around the theory that 'the bomber will always get through', and

The 'Stuka' dive bomber—tested in the Spanish Civil War by the Kondor Legion and then used with devastating effect in German offensives in World War II.

> **I believe that the double policy of rearmament, and better relations with Germany and Italy will carry us safely through the danger period.**
>
> *Neville Chamberlain, 1937.*

the RAF got priority. Chamberlain fully supported rearmament, and this is often forgotten. But he was essentially a man of peace, who had been a successful Health Minister and Chancellor of the Exchequer. He wanted to spend most of Britain's money on new housing and schools. He also thought that the dictators were rather like badly behaved trade union leaders. It should be possible to get them talking around a table. Above all Chamberlain remembered the terrible slaughter in World War One, in which his own cousin Norman had died. It is easy to think that the appeasers were cowards. They weren't. The problem was that Hitler *wasn't* just an angry trade union leader.

> **... The Treaty of Versailles was fallible and hence an unjust basis on which to build up a permanent settlement of Eastern Europe.**
>
> *Neville Henderson, British Ambassador to Berlin, 1937.*

It is important to understand appeasement, because Hitler's success after 1936 owed a good deal to the belief that it would work.

THE HOSSBACH MEMORANDUM

1937 was an 'off year' for Hitler. There were no 'Saturday surprises'. But there was a very important meeting in Hitler's Berlin Chancellery in November. The minutes were taken by a Colonel Hossbach, and so the record of the meeting is usually known as the 'Hoss-

bach Memorandum'. All the important German leaders were there. At the meeting Hitler said two important things: 1) Germany must be ready to fight a major war *before* 1943. After that her enemies would be too strong. 2) She must be ready 'to overthrow Czechoslovakia and Austria simultaneously'. Remember that the former had a German minority of 3 million, and the latter was a German speaking country.

> **Nobody knew today what the situation would be in the years 1943–45. One thing only was certain, that we could not wait longer.**
>
> *Adolf Hitler as recorded in the Hossbach Memorandum, 1937.*

The Hossbach Memorandum was clear evidence of Hitler's aggressive plans. A copy of it was used at the trials of the Nazi leaders by the Allies in 1946.

THE ANSCHLUSS

As an Austrian himself, Hitler had always taken the keenest interest in the fate of his homeland. But the Treaty of Versailles as we have seen prevented union between Austria and Germany (the German word for union is *anschluss*). This was another part of the treaty that the Führer didn't intend to keep. First of all he bullied the Austrian Chancellor Schuschnigg in an interview at his mountain house at Berchtesgaden. The chain smoking Schuschnigg wasn't allowed to smoke and a general was stationed outside the door. The terrified Austrian Chancellor was only allowed to go when he agreed to a ten point ultimatum. A Nazi supporter Seyss Inquart would control the Austrian police, and there would be Nazis in the Austrian army.

> **I may be in Vienna overnight like a storm in the spring! Then you will experience something.**
>
> *Hitler to von Schuschnigg, 12 February 1938.*

Surprisingly, when he got home (and recovered his nerve) Schuschnigg dared to defy Hitler. He couldn't get any support from Britain or France, and Austria's old friend Mussolini said she was now 'a German problem'. But Schuschnigg decided to hold a *plebiscite* or yes/no vote. Did the Austrian people want union with Germany or not? The date set for the vote was Sunday March 13 1938. Hitler couldn't allow this vote to take place: he might have lost it! So over the Friday night and Saturday morning, German troops entered Austria. The Anschluss only

> **Spring manoeuvres.**
>
> *Hitler's London ambassador Ribbentrop's explanation for German troop movements before the Anschluss.*

got paper protests from Britain and France. Eight million Austrians now became part of Hitler's 'Thousand Year Reich'. Yet again he had got away with breaking the peace treaty.

> **I believe that it was God's will to send a boy from here into the Reich, to let him grow up, to raise him to leader of the nation so as to enable him to lead his homeland into the Reich.**
>
> *Hitler in Vienna, 1938.*

After Austria had been absorbed, Hitler's gaze turned towards Czechoslovakia (although as the Hossbach document makes

clear he would have taken Czechoslovakia and Austria *together* if the opportunity had arisen). The map on page 59 will show you how vulnerable Czechoslovakia had become after the Anschluss. It was now surrounded on three sides by German land. Hitler of course was especially interested in the Sudetenland, the area where 3 million Germans lived. But it had never been part of Germany before the First World War, so in this case Hitler wasn't just revising the Versailles Treaty.

THE CZECH CRISIS

Soon after the Anschluss Hitler started up a big propaganda campaign against the Czechs. Their leader Beneš was accused of deliberately ill-treating Sudeten Germans, and a Sudeten German party under Konrad Henlein (a former PE teacher) demanded self government. The Nazis were very good at telling lies, and many people in Britain believed them.

> **More and more Sudeten Germans were terrorized by one method or another into joining the Sudeten German Party.**
>
> *Elizabeth Wiskemann, The Rome-Berlin Axis*

As Hitler's anti-Czech speeches became more and more warlike the British prime minister became worried. He sent Lord Runciman to the Sudetenland in September on a fact finding mission. But Runciman was easily tricked by Henlein, who is now known to have been taking his orders direct from Berlin. So the British took German claims about Czech 'atrocities' in the Sudetenland at face value.

BERCHTESGADEN

As Hitler continued to make threats Chamberlain decided to intervene in person. In mid September he flew to meet Hitler at his mountain house in Berchtesgaden. This was a brave thing for an old man of sixty-nine who had never flown before to do. Hitler was not in a very friendly mood. He insisted that the Sudeten Germans be given *autonomy* or home rule. Chamberlain thought he could persuade the French to agree (he knew the French would). If need be Britain would threaten to desert Czechoslovakia if she wouldn't agree.

GODESBURG

A week later Chamberlain flew back to Germany. This time Hitler came down to the Rhineland town of Godesburg. To reduce the

Hitler and Mussolini.

Neville Chamberlain, British prime minister, with Hitler.

old man's journey (he claimed). When Chamberlain arrived he had a shock. Having persuaded the reluctant Czechs to accept the Berchtesgaden terms, he now found Hitler had raised the stakes. The Czechs had to be out of the Sudetenland by 1 October 1938, and Hungarian and Polish claims against them had to be accepted too. Even Chamberlain was angered by this piece of deception on Hitler's part. He returned to London to talk to his colleagues.

War seemed inevitable. The French army entered the forts of its great Maginot line. Trenches were dug in Hyde Park and gas masks given out. The Royal Navy was put on action stations. Chamberlain talked in shocked tones of war, 'for a faraway country of which we know nothing'.

The British prime minister approached Mussolini for help. The Italian dictator then persuaded his friend Hitler to attend a conference about the Sudetenland. While Chamberlain spoke in the House of Commons, he arranged for a note to be passed to him with the news.

> **'Thank God for the prime minister.'**
> *Hysterical MPs greet the news of the Munich Conference, 1938*

After the successful reoccupation of the Rhineland and the 'Anschluss' with Austria it was

Czechoslovakia's turn. Hitler enters the capital of the Sudetenland in 1938.

MUNICH

A 4 Power conference (Britain, France, Germany, Italy) was to be held in the South German city of Munich, where Hitler began his political career. The Russians weren't invited. Neither were the Czechs. Their representatives had to wait in a nearby hotel, while their country was carved up. Critics of the Munich agreement took it as a sign when the inkwell to sign it was found to be empty! It gave Hitler the Sudetenland without a shot. With it came the Czech frontier fortifications (which impressed German generals). But Hitler was annoyed. It seems that he really did want war and complained that Chamberlain had 'spoilt my entry into Prague'. Nevertheless he agreed to meet with Chamberlain in his Munich flat and sign a special 'Anglo-German Declaration'.

Neville Chamberlain returns to England with the Anglo-German declaration.

Both sides promised to avoid war in future. Chamberlain told the crowds that it was 'peace in our time'. Hitler claimed he had signed the declaration to please 'the old gentleman'. At the time Chamberlain was a hero. His fans included US President Roosevelt who sent him the two word telegram 'good man'.

Was Munich a mistake? Perhaps. While it allowed Britain a year to develop radar and Spitfires, it gave Hitler a year to build up his forces too. Chamberlain knew Britain had only 12 anti-aircraft guns in September 1938, but Munich made Czechoslovakia defenceless. The Russian dictator Stalin also feared that the West was ganging up with Hitler against him.

Let us say of the Munich Settlement that it was inescapable. Mr Chamberlain had no alternative to do other than he did.

John Wheeler Bennett, 'Munich. Prologue to Tragedy'.

THE END OF CZECHOSLOVAKIA

The hopes that Munich might preserve the peace proved to be false. Hitler had no intention of keeping it, although he didn't yet want a war with Britain and France. But the temptation to seize the rest of defenceless Czechoslovakia was too great for him. Neither did he believe that 'the little worms' (i.e. Britain and France) of Munich would stop him. On 15 March German forces entered Czechoslovakia after Hitler had bullied the Czech President Hácha into accepting them (at one point in the interview he fainted and had to be revived by a morphine injection). Independent Czechoslovakia disappeared from the map, and Germany got a great haul of excellent Czech tanks and guns.

Now even Chamberlain realized something had to be done, although he didn't give up his hopes that Germany might be 'appeased'. When a week later Hitler seized the German speaking port of Memel from Lithuania, Chamberlain decided to act. A guarantee of help was given to Poland if Germany attacked her. Further guarantees were given to Romania, Greece, and Turkey. Britain would fight for Poland when she wouldn't fight for Czechoslovakia. Meantime Hitler's friend Mussolini grabbed the tiny kingdom of Albania on Good Friday 1939. He was envious of German success. Poland was clearly next in line. Throughout the summer of 1939 Hitler demanded the return of Danzig and the Corridor. Poland wouldn't budge.

THE PACT OF STEEL

Italy took another big step into the German camp in May 1939, when she signed the so-called 'Pact of Steel'. Unlike the Rome-Berlin Axis of 1936, this *was* a military agreement.

Both Italy and Germany signed a 10 year agreement, each promising to help the other if it were attacked.

THE NAZI-SOVIET PACT

The big mystery in the months leading up to World War Two—was what would Stalin do? After Munich Stalin became suspicious of the West, and in March 1939 he made an important speech to the Communist Party Congress in Moscow. It is sometimes called Stalin's 'chestnuts speech' because in it he warned other states not to count on the

Soviet Union to 'pull their chestnuts out of the fire' for them.

This was a clear warning to France and Britain. But it wasn't heeded. Britain sent negotiators to Moscow, but they went by sea, taking a week. This didn't impress Stalin or his new Foreign Minister Molotov (later nicknamed 'Mr No' by foreign journalists). They wanted to know if the Red Army would be allowed into Poland, if Germany attacked. Britain and France couldn't answer that one. They knew the Poles wouldn't agree. Stalin grew impatient. On 23 August 1939, after quickly inviting German Foreign Minister Ribbentrop to Moscow, he signed a non-aggression treaty with Nazi Germany. The treaty also said (in a secret clause) that Poland would be divided up.

Everyone in the West was stunned. It was as if the Pope had made an agreement with the Devil. Hitler plainly thought he had played his ace card. 'Now I have got them,' he boasted. He couldn't believe that Britain and France would fight without Russia. But he was wrong.

> **I know how much the German nation loves its Führer; I should therefore like to drink his health.**
>
> Josef Stalin to Foreign Minister von Ribbentrop on 23 August 1939.

Instead the British guarantee to Poland became a military agreement. Momentarily Hitler postponed his invasion plan. He consulted his Italian allies, but Mussolini said he wasn't ready to fight. He sent Hitler a long list of arms needed by Italy, which Italian Foreign Minister Ciano said 'would kill a bull, if a bull could read'. This bull could read, and he realized he would have to fight alone. But

the planning of 'Case White' (the codename for the invasion of Poland) went ahead. Meantime peace messages flew across Europe. The Pope, the Queen of Holland, President Roosevelt, and various Swedish friends of Goering were all involved. But it was useless. Hitler was determined to have his war, and on 1 September Germany invaded Poland. Two days later after Hitler had ignored their warnings, Britain and France declared war on Germany.

> **Everything I have worked for, everything I have hoped for ... has crashed into ruins.**
>
> Neville Chamberlain to the British people in his radio broadcast of 3 September 1939.

WHOSE RESPONSIBILITY WAS IT?

There has been a good deal of argument amongst historians about responsibility for the Second World War since it ended in 1945. Before 1961 most historians went along with the view that the war was really 'Hitler's War'. But in that year A. J. P. Taylor brought out his book *The Origins of The Second World War*, which stirred up a hornet's nest! Taylor largely dismissed what Hitler said in *Mein Kampf*, and said that the Hossbach Memorandum didn't matter because every country had war plans. Taylor went on to say that: 'The vital question it seems to me, concerns Great Britain and France. They had the decision in their hands.' It was Britain and France, said Taylor, rather than Hitler who were mainly to blame for starting the war. Infuriatingly (for other historians) Taylor said that the appeasement policy hadn't been carried *far enough*.

COUNTDOWN TO WAR

1933 Hitler in power. Germany leaves the League.

1934 German Polish non aggression treaty.
Murder of Dollfuss.

1935 Stresa front. Mussolini invades Abyssinia.
Anglo-German Naval Treaty.

1936 Hitler reoccupies Rhineland.
Spanish Civil War starts.
Rome-Berlin Axis.

1937 Hossbach Memorandum. Anti-Comintern Pact,
Chamberlain prime minister.

1938 Austro-German Anschluss.
Czech crisis and Munich Conference.

1939 Hitler occupies Czechoslovakia.
Pact of Steel.
Nazi-Soviet pact.
German attack on Poland.

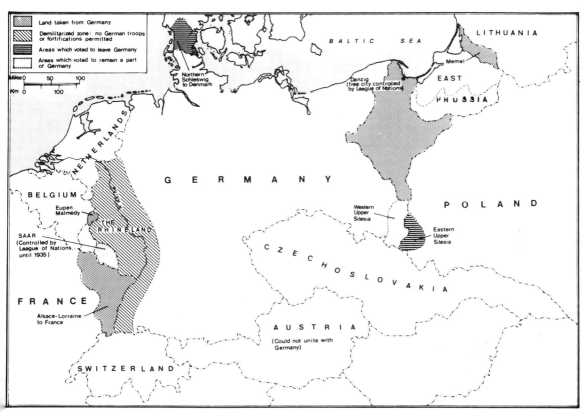

Map showing the effects of the Treaty of Versailles (1919) on German territory.

CONCLUSION

WHAT THE THIRD REICH MEANT FOR THE GERMAN PEOPLE

When Germany went to war in September 1939, her people were not enthusiastic about it. There were no cheering crowds in the streets as there had been in 1914, when the First World War started. Yet in April 1945 when Russian tanks were a street away from Hitler's underground bunker, twelve-year-old boys were still fighting desperately for the Third Reich. Why? Partly it was because Germans were a naturally patriotic people. But this last ditch resistance was also a result of the fact that a majority of the German people continued to believe in Hitler until the end of the war.

In Westphalia a flat tyre forced us to stop. Unrecognized in the twilight I stood in a farm-yard talking to farmers. To my surprise, the faith in Hitler which had been hammered into their minds all these last years was still strong. Hitler could never lose the war, they declared, 'The Führer is still holding something in reserve that he'll play at the last moment. Then the turning point will come. It's only a trap, his letting the enemy come so far into our country.'

Albert Speer, Memoirs

Even in the early part of the War when Germany was winning great victories, conditions at home were tough. Hot water was allowed only two days a week, and many Germans found it almost impossible to get ordinary things like clothes and shoes.

All Germans were given ration books. They had to exist on a diet of vegetables, black rye bread with a little meat, butter, and just one egg a week. Women suffered particularly badly because not only were they expected to do war work in factories, but also to run a house *and* queue for hours to get foodstuffs. Evidence available to historians shows that in 1939–40 many German women were being diagnosed by doctors as suffering from exhaustion and depression.

The important point here was that Germany, unlike Britain, began rationing of *all* foodstuffs from the start of the war. Hitler apparently thought that everyone should be made to sacrifice something for the Reich. This produced a good deal of grumbling, but no collapse of fighting spirit.

'What is the difference between India and Germany? In India, one man starves for all, in Germany all starve for one man!' German joke comparing Hitler and the Indian leader Gandhi in 1939–40. Gandhi often went on fasts.

This remained true throughout the war. Cities like Berlin, Dresden, and Hamburg were devastated by Allied bombing. But never did the morale of the civilian population crack. Instead, most Germans went on hoping that their Führer would produce new secret weapons to win the war. And, of course, he nearly did. As we have seen, Germany almost had an atomic bomb in 1945, and already had ballistic missiles and jet fighters.

All this self-sacrifice was for nothing in the end. Seven million Germans died in Hitler's war, and many cities and towns were little more than piles of rubble. Germany was to be occupied by Britain, France, the USA and the USSR for many years after 1945, and did not become a united country again until 1989. And she took the blame for Hitler's crimes in which so many Germans had co-operated.

In the end, Hitler cared nothing for the German people. They had 'failed' him and did not deserve their Führer. So orders were given to blow up anything of value. Hitler wanted to take the German people down with him.

The 'Thousand Year Reich' had lasted for just twelve years. Throughout its history from the 'Night of the Long Knives' to the Holocaust, it had been about the barbaric and inhuman treatment of human beings. After 1945, Germans had to live with the memory of what the Third Reich had done in their name.

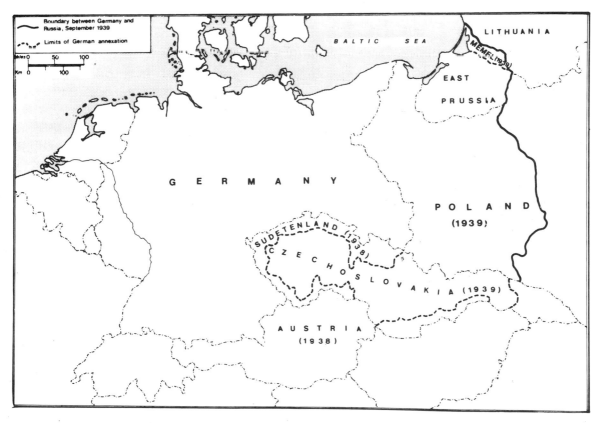

Map showing the expansion of German territory between 1938 and 1939.

FURTHER READING

†Shirer, W. *Berlin Diary, Rise and Fall of the Third Reich*, Pan, 1960

†Bielenberg, Christobel, *The Past is Myself*, Corgi, 1989

†*Signal*, Hitler's Wartime Picture Magazine, Bison, 1976

†*Ann Frank's Diary*

*J. F. Aylett, *Hitler's Germany*, Hodder, 1992

†*The Goebbels Diaries: The Last Days*, Pan, 1979

†Speer, Albert *Inside the Third Reich*, Weidenfeld, 1970

*Richardson, N. How and Why? The Third Reich, Batsford 1987

*Ross, S. *Racism in The Third Reich*, Batsford, 1992

*Howarth, T. & Brooman, J. *Twentieth Century History* (Ch. 23), Longman, 1987 2nd Edition.

* = GCSE style books
† = Primary source material and secondary

INDEX

INDEX